I0763197

Mi mundo / Inside My World

MI DÍA EN LA ESCUELA/ MY DAY AT SCHOOL

By Tina Benjamin

Traducido por Charlotte Bockman

Please visit our website, www.garethstevens.com. For a free color catalog of all our high-quality books, call toll free 1-800-542-2595 or fax 1-877-542-2596.

Library of Congress Cataloging-in-Publication Data

Benjamin, Tina.
My day at school = Mi día en la escuela / by Tina Benjamin.
pages cm. — (Inside my world = Mi Mundo)
Parallel title: Mi Mundo.
In English and Spanish.
Includes index.
ISBN 978-1-4824-2360-0 (library binding)
1. Schools — Juvenile literature. 2. School day — Juvenile literature. I. Benjamin, Tina. II. Title.
LB1513.B45 2015
372—d23

First Edition

Published in 2015 by
Gareth Stevens Publishing
111 East 14th Street, Suite 349
New York, NY 10003

Editor: Nathalie Beullens-Maoui
Designer: Sarah Liddell
Spanish Translation: Charlotte Bockman

Photo credits: Cover, p. 1 Brocreative/Shutterstock.com; p. 5 littleny/Shutterstock.com; pp. 7, 9, 21 Hurst Photo/Shutterstock.com; pp. 11, 24 (desk) sdecoret/Shutterstock.com; pp. 13, 15, 17 Monkey Business Images/Shutterstock.com; pp. 19, 24 (basketball) Robert Kneschke/Shutterstock.com; p. 23 rSnapshotPhotos/Shutterstock.com.

Printed in the United States of America

CPSIA compliance information: Batch #CW15GS: For further information contact Gareth Stevens, New York, New York at 1-800-542-2595.

Contenido

Contents

Hoy es lunes.
¡Voy a la escuela!

Today is Monday.
I am going
to school today!

Tengo una
mochila azul.
Llevo los libros en ella.

I have a blue backpack.
I carry my books in it.

Voy en el autobús
de la escuela.
Me siento
con mi amiga Liza.

I ride on a school bus.
I sit with my friend Liza.

Vamos a clase.
¡Tengo mi
propio pupitre!

We go to class.
I have my own desk!

Me gusta mi maestra.

I like my teacher.

Nos enseña
acerca de los animales.

She teaches us
about animals.

Es hora de almorzar.
Me gusta comer
con mis amigos.

I go to lunch.
I love to eat lunch
with my friends.

Voy al gimnasio.
¡Jugamos baloncesto!

I go to gym.
We play basketball!

Regreso a casa
en el autobús.

I take the bus
home, too.

SCHOOL DIST.

El conductor me deja
en mi casa.
¡Por hoy, terminó
la escuela!

The bus driver drops me
off at my house.
My school day is over!

SCHOOL BUS
EMERGENCY DOOR
SLOW

Palabras que debes saber/ Words to Know

(el) baloncesto/ basketball

(el) pupitre/ desk

Índice/Index